Filippo Pedrocco

TIEPOLO

SCALA

CONTENTS

Photographs: SCALA ARCHIVE
except nos. 1, 2, 23, 46, 58 (Osvaldo Böhm, Venice); nos. 3, 24, 25
(by courtesy of the author); nos. 5, 33, 37, 38, 39, 40 (Umberto
Marzani, Milan); nos. 7, 9 (by courtesy of the National Gallery of Art,
Washington); nos. 11, 12, 13, 14, 15, 16, 17 (Elio Ciol, Pordenone);
nos. 18, 19, 59 (by courtesy of the Metropolitan Museum of Art, New
York); no. 31 (Universitet Konsthistoriska Institutionen, Stockholm);
nos. 34, 82 (by courtesy of the National Gallery, London); no. 42
(by courtesy of the Stanley Moss Collection, Riverdale on Hudson/
New York); no. 45 (by courtesy of the Art Institute, Chicago); no. 60
(Szépmüvészeti Museum, Budapest); no. 81 (Charles Potter Kling
Fund, by courtesy of the Museum of Fine Arts, Boston); no. 84 (by
courtesy of the Ashmolean Museum, Oxford); no. 87 (Museu
Nacional de Arte Antigua, Lisbon); no. 88 (Staatsgalerie, Stuttgart)

Editing: Marilena Vecchi
Translation: Christopher Evans

Printed in Italy by: Arti Grafiche "Stampa Nazionale", Calenzano
(Florence), 1996

Early Experiences

Giambattista Tiepolo was born on March 5, 1696, in Corte San Domenico, in the heavily populated Venetian quarter of Castello. The fact that the nobleman Giovanni Donà served as godfather at his baptism, celebrated on April 16 in the cathedral church of San Pietro, has often been regarded as proof of the kinship of the Tiepolo family of Corte San Domenico with the glorious and noble house of Tiepolo that had provided the Serenissima with doges, patriarchs and procurators of St. Mark. But it is a hypothesis that has no grounds in reality: the fact is that Giambattista's father, Domenico, was in the shipping business. Owning a part-share in a number of trading vessels, he had dedicated himself with some success to maritime trade. There is no trace of his name in any of the numerous patrician genealogies of eighteenth- and nineteenth-century Venice. His untimely death, in the March of 1697, left the responsibility for the maintenance of his large family in the hands of his wife, Orsetta Marangon. For many years she had to cope with considerable financial hardship, as she was unable to recoup the investments made by her husband.

So Giambattista was born and raised in an environment that had nothing to do with the world of art. And yet in 1710 he joined the studio of one of the best-known artists in Venice at the time, Gregorio Lazzarini. The young Tiepolo spent a long time with the only teacher he ever had: in fact his name was not recorded in the Fraglia, the guild of Venetian painters, until 1717, which means that he had not left Lazzarini's studio until that time.

It has often been asked what the real significance of Lazzarini's teaching was and the majority of art historians have assumed that Gregorio did no more than instill the technical rudiments of the painter's craft in his young and brilliant pupil: drawing, perspective, and the ability to fill compositions of a large size with a large number of figures, arranged in grandiose and magniloquent forms.

Yet it is likely that the situation was quite different, for the seven or eight years spent by Giambattista in Lazzarini's studio was a considerable period of time, certainly far too long for Tiepolo to have been engaged in learning no more than the practical aspects of painting. On the contrary, these were decisive years for the

1. Memento mori
11.5x9 cm
Venice, Gallerie dell'Accademia

artist, which he used to build up the vast store of visual knowledge that he was to utilize, reworking it and adapting it to his own needs of expression, over the course of his very long career.

The same significance can be attached to one of the very first commissions received by Giambattista, that of making graphic reproductions of a number of paintings by sixteenth-century artists – Tintoretto, Francesco Bassano, and Giuseppe Salviati – for the collection of engravings that make up the *Gran Teatro delle pitture e prospettive di Venezia*, published by Domenico Lovisa in 1717. This lowly work as a copier must certainly have allowed the young painter to gain a mastery of the compositional structures and figurative elements that he was required to reproduce. And this continual interest in study was something that he was to retain throughout his life: in March 1762, just a few days before he left Venice on a journey to Madrid from which he would never return, Giambattista, now over sixty years old, gave a sort of interview to the *Nuova Veneta Gazzetta* in which he briefly summed up the philosophy of his artistic career. Among other things, he stated that "the Painter's life should be one of constant study." And it certainly cannot be denied that Tiepolo kept to this rule for the whole of his life. In fact, right from his earliest works, Giambattista showed that he had studied the works of numerous other artists with great attention. These included pictures by his contemporaries, from Federico Bencovich to Giambattista Piazzetta, Sebastiano Ricci to Dorigny, Andrea Celesti to Bellucci, Segala, Bambini, Molinari, and the Lombard Paolo Pagani, as well as by many seventeenth-century painters, from Giulio Carpioni to Loth and Zanchi, and by the great masters of the sixteenth century, in particular Tintoretto and Paolo Veronese, though he did not neglect Jacopo Bassano, Titian, and Salviati. Thus his earliest works already reveal his great capacity to look around him, to absorb stimuli and ideas from the paintings of a variety of artists and then go on to rework them to meet the needs of his own sensibility. This was a practice that he shared with Lazzarini.

"Though he departed from his [Gregorio Lazzarini's] diligent manner, in that [he was] all spirit and fire, and embraced a fluent and decisive style," wrote Vincenzo Da Canal, Lazzarini's biographer, of Tiepolo in 1732. It is true that Giambattista's juvenile works confirm the considerable difference in style between pupil and master, evident in the adoption by the younger artist of a rapid and confident technique of painting, undoubtedly in keeping with his character. This would permit him, as he continued with his career, to carry out the fresco decoration of vast spaces in churches, palaces, and villas at an incredible speed.

Another element is immediately apparent from an examination of some of his earliest works, whose authenticity is testified by contemporary sources. The five ornamental panels painted between 1715 and 1716, to be placed above the arches of the Venetian church of the Ospedaletto and depicting pairs of *Apostles*, are characterized by dark tones of color and a dramatic handling of light, in a manner that is strongly reminiscent of the work of the *tenebrosi* (i.e. late baroque) painters, especially Federico Bencovich and Giambattista Piazzetta. On the other hand, the *Portraits of Doges Marco and Giovanni II Cornaro*, painted for the family palace of the incumbent doge, probably in 1716, are distinguished by their warm colors, in light shades, and recall the style of Sebastiano Ricci. Apart from the different intonation of color, however, what is common to these early paintings is their incisive touch, with sharp outlines, and the richness of the free and vibrant brushwork.

So Giambattista showed himself capable of moving in different stylistic directions, perhaps partly in deference to the wishes of his clients. And this aspect of Tiepolo's art also has to be seen as a consequence of the young painter's apprenticeship with Lazzarini: Gregorio was an eclectic artist, and his curriculum is marked by a great diversity of artistic experiences. A pupil of the *tenebroso* Francesco Rosa, who was a fine exponent of the dramatic style developed by the Genoese, though Venetian by adoption, painter Giambattista

2. The Apostles Thomas and John
205x390 cm
Venice, church of the Ospedaletto

Langetti, Lazzarini also seems to have been fully aware of the great Venetian pictorial tradition of the cinquecento, and in particular the examples set by Tintoretto and Veronese. But what appears to be his most significant characteristic is his flexibility, his ability to adopt different styles to suit the subject on which he was working. It is a characteristic shared, as we have seen, by the young Tiepolo.

Perhaps it was in part through the good offices of the well-established Lazzarini, who had been able to build up an extensive network of relations at home and abroad over the course of his long and industrious life, that Giambattista obtained his first major commissions: at the Ospedaletto and in the house of the doge then in office, Giovanni II Cornaro, where – according to Da Canal – "he presided over the arrangement of pictorial things" and at the same time painted "several ornamental panels with portraits and pictures in good taste."

However he painted pictures for other clients too during the initial phase of his career. Da Canal tells us that on the feast day of St. Rock, August 16, 1716, Giambattista had exhibited – to considerable acclaim – a canvas depicting the *Drowning of the Pharaoh*. This was probably a study for a work of larger size intended for the church of Santi Cosma e Damiano on Giudecca. The small canvas was rediscovered by Egidio Martini in 1964 but, unfortunately, is now in an inaccessible private collection. Nevertheless it is apparent from photographs that it already had well-defined stylistic features, with dark and glowing shades of color and a dramatic handling of light. These are qualities reminiscent of the contemporary school of *tenebrosi*, and of Bencovich and Piazzetta in particular. Identical characteristics are to be seen in the small oval painting on copper depicting a *Memento mori* that was donated to the Gallerie dell'Accademia of Venice in 1968 by Antonio Morassi, one of the greatest experts on Tiepolo. It is a work of intense drama, underlined by the harshness of color and the spiky and uneven texture of the brushwork.

The fact that he had been given the post of painter to the current doge must have opened up considerable opportunities for the young Tiepolo. In 1716 he began his activity as a fresco painter, working first on the *Assumption* in the parish church of Biadene and shortly afterward, in 1719-20, on the decoration of the salon on the second floor of a villa at Massanzago, in the vicinity of Padua. This belonged to the extremely wealthy publisher Giovan Battista Baglioni, who had recently been raised to the Venetian nobility thanks to his ritual payment of a hundred thousand ducats into the empty coffers of the Venetian Republic. His collaborator on the perspective wall paintings was the Ferrarese artist Gerolamo Mengozzi, known as Colonna, who was to be his faithful companion on numerous other occasions over the years to come.

In the frescoes at Massanzago Giambattista shows that he had already developed the scheme of decoration that he was to use so often over the course of his career, as it proved particularly agreeable to his clients: the frescoes cover the room completely, creating the illusion that its walls have vanished and been replaced by an unbounded space. The *Triumph of Aurora* appears on the ceiling, while the *Myth of Phaëthon*, the first version of a theme that he was to tackle frequently, is depicted on the walls. The colors, in this case, are lighter and brighter.

Along with frescoes in Venice (*Saint Jerome pointing at the Cross* in the sacristy of the church of San Giovanni Crisostomo and *The Apotheosis of Saint Theresa* in the second chapel on the right of the church of the Scalzi) and at Vascon near Treviso (*The Glory of Saint Lucy* on the ceiling of the parish church, dating from 1722), Giambattista also painted several pictures on canvas during this period. After *The Repudiation of Vasti*, now in a private collection in Milan, in 1719, he produced a number of large historical or religious scenes. The finest of these is undoubtedly the astonishing *Madonna del Carmelo*, painted for a chapel of the Venetian church of Sant'Aponal, which after a series of strange adventures turned up at Brera in 1925, split in two. The large canvas had been commissioned from him by the pharmacist Giacomo Toni on December 1, 1721. However Giambattista, even though he painted the greater part of it at once, did not deliver the picture until 1727. He took

great care over the composition, taking into account the fact that it was to be hung on a side wall of the chapel, under unusual conditions of lighting and visibility. Thus the figure of the Virgin handing the scapular to St. Simon Stock – which certainly owes a debt to the one painted by Paolo Veronese for the *San Zaccaria Altarpiece* – does not occupy the center of the scene, but is displaced to the right. The left-hand side of the painting (the part that was cut off during the nineteenth century, precisely to remedy the fact that the figure of the Virgin was not in the middle) is devoted to a dramatic vision of souls in Purgatory, with a large winged angel indicating the way of salvation through devotion to Mary. The dark and smoky colors impart an atmosphere of high drama to the scene, which is very similar to the one portrayed in the contemporary – and unfortunately badly damaged – *Crucifixion of Saint Martin* on Burano.

The coloring is quite different in the delightful series of four small mythological canvases in Venice's Gallerie dell'Accademia, in which the notable plasticity of the figures is softened by the progressive lightening of the palette. The same characteristics are present in an accentuated form in the series of large canvases depicting *Scenes from the Life of Queen Zenobia*, which were probably painted around this time (Da Canal describes them as "one of his earliest compositions") for Palazzo Zenobio at the Carmini. These are now split up among a number of different locations (National Gallery of Washington, Gal-

3. The Triumph of Aurora Massanzago (Padua), Villa Baglioni

4. Portrait of Doge Marco Cornaro 271x182 cm Venice, private collection

5. Madonna del Carmelo
210x650 cm
Milan, Pinacoteca
Nazionale di Brera

leria Sabauda in Turin, and Museo del Prado in Madrid, while two large fragments of the fourth canvas are in the Crespi Collection in Milan). In some of them the luminosity becomes downright radiant: this is particularly true of the scene of *Zenobia addressing her Soldiers*, now in Washington, with the result that critics have often dated this work to the following decade, even though it is unquestionably contemporary with the rest of the cycle.

The *Martyrdom of Saint Bartholomew* in the church of San Stae dates from 1722 and belongs to a set of twelve canvases depicting episodes from the lives of the apostles in which each picture was painted by a celebrated artist of the time. They were originally intended, in accordance with the last will and testament of the patrician Andrea Stazio, to decorate the nave of the church. It was only later that they were transferred to the presbytery and surrounded by stuccoes, where they can still be seen. Perhaps stimulated by the confrontation with Piazzetta, author of one of the pictures in the series,

Giambattista returns to a more dramatic style and greater contrasts in this painting. The figure of the martyred saint, caught in a beam of bright light from above, stands out with extraordinary violence from the dark background, unlike those of his assassins. One of these is derived from a painting by Solimena that was then in the possession of the same Giambattista Baglioni who had commissioned him to paint the frescoes at Massanzago.

There is a close parallel between the *Martyrdom of Saint Bartholomew* and the last of the ornamental panels in the Ospedaletto representing the *Sacrifice of Isaac*, painted in 1724 at the time when the Ticinese architect Domenico Rossi was making alterations to the internal structure of the building. The chronological proximity of these pictures is confirmed beyond any possible doubt by the identical shades of color and handling of light. Another significant piece of evidence is the fact that Tiepolo appears to have used the same model for the figures of St. Bartholomew and Isaac.

6. Martyrdom of Saint Bartholomew
167x139 cm
Venice, church of San Stae

7, 9. Queen Zenobia addressing her Soldiers
261.4x365.8 cm
Washington, National Gallery of Art

8. The Triumph of Aurelianus
260x402 cm
Turin, Galleria Sabauda

Toward Maturity: the Frescoes in the Palazzo Patriarcale in Udine

It was probably at the Ospedaletto that Giambattista commenced the working partnership with Domenico Rossi that was to last until the end of the 1720s. This was a period that covered the years in which the painter made his definitive choice of field, progressively abandoning the world of the *tenebrosi* and developing his style based on brilliant colors and light tones, bathed in a radiant, Apollonian light. Unfortunately we know little about the personality of Rossi, an architect with a solid grounding in baroque culture but not insensitive to the decorative refinements of the rococo style, and are therefore unable to tell what influence he may have exercised on the evolution of Tiepolo's style in these years. But the fact that Rossi had often collaborated with the Frenchman Louis Dorigny, i.e. one of the first artists in Veneto to move away from the style of the *tenebrosi* and toward paler, brighter shades of color and an accentuated formal elegance, may be considered an interesting indication of the architect's taste and suggest that more importance should be attached to this relationship than has been hitherto.

In 1724-25 Giambattista painted *The Triumph of Eloquence* on the ceiling of the salon on the *piano nobile* of Palazzo Sandi, which had just been rebuilt by Rossi. The subject was obviously intended to exalt the virtues of the client, Tommaso Sandi, a celebrated Venetian advocate. In this outstanding work Giambattista isolated the figures of Minerva, goddess of Wisdom, and Mercury, god of Eloquence, at the center of the ceiling. On each of the four sides of the molding he set an episode from mythology (*Orpheus guiding Eurydice out of Hades*; *Hercules Gallicus chaining one of the Cercops by its Tongue*; *Bellerophon mounted on Pegasus killing the Chimera*; *Amphion, by the Power of Music, causes the Walls of Thebes to build Themselves*). This scheme of composition is close to the one often adopted by the great baroque decorators, and in particular by Luca Giordano for the ceiling of Palazzo Medici Riccardi in Florence. It is not impossible that the young Tiepolo had heard about these works from Dorigny. As has already been pointed out, Dorigny had been a close collaborator of Rossi's and had had the opportunity to study these models at first hand on his visits to the major artistic centers of Italy.

In the fresco in Palazzo Sandi Tiepolo defined the structure of a composition that he was to repeat innumerable times in similar decorative undertakings: at the center of the scene, against a blue sky flecked with clouds, he would arrange a few figures, at times gods and he-

roes of mythology, at others sacred personages; around the edge he would place a crowd of secondary figures, whose role was to witness the event and underline its significance. But there is another reason why *The Triumph of Eloquence* is particularly important: it shows that Giambattista was coming decisively under the influence of Veronese. This is apparent not only in the lightening of his palette, but also in the eighteenth-century painter's adoption of a technique typical of Paolo, the use of colored shadows. In the scene from the legend of Amphion, for example, he placed a youth gazing downward alongside the mythological hero: on the youth's face we can see the reflection of the ash-blue light coming from the blue cloak worn by Amphion.

The influence of Veronese is equally apparent in the three canvases of mythological subjects painted for the same room: in the one depicting *Ulysses discovering Achilles among the Daughters of Lycomedes*, now along with the other two in a private collection in Vicenza, this is revealed by the coloristic and decorative effect of the fabrics of the women's clothing, richly woven out of luminous silks and precious damasks.

With the work on Palazzo Sandi over, Giambattista went to Udine, where he first frescoed the vault of the chapel of the Holy Sacrament in the cathedral and, immediately afterward, started on the decoration of the Palazzo Patriarcale: both these buildings had been restored and restructured by Domenico Rossi.

Giambattista worked in the palace – to a commission from the Venetian Dionisio Dolfin, patriarch of Aquileia – from 1726 to 1729. First he painted the fresco on the ceiling of the grand staircase, depicting *The Fall of the Rebel Angels*. Then he moved on to the gallery, where he painted some scenes from the lives of the Biblical patriarchs on the walls (*The Appearance of the Angels to Abraham*, *Rachel hiding the Idols*; *The Appearance of the Angel to Sarah*), interspersed with monochrome figures of *Prophetesses*, and *The Sacrifice of Isaac* and two tondi representing *Jacob's Dream* and *Agar comforted by the Angel* on the ceiling. Next, in the Sala Rossa, then the seat of the ecclesiastical court, he painted the emblematic *Judgment of Solomon*, surrounded by the figures of the Major Prophets, Isaiah, Jeremiah, Ezekiel, and Daniel. Finally, in the Throne Room, he frescoed a

10. The Triumph of Eloquence
650x1070 cm
Venice, Palazzo Sandi

11, 13. *Rachel hiding the Idols*
Udine, Palazzo Patriarcale

12. *The Appearance of the Angels to Abraham*
Udine, Palazzo Patriarcale

14. *The Appearance of the Angel to Sarah*
Udine, Palazzo Patriarcale

15. *The Sacrifice of Isaac*
Udine, Palazzo Patriarcale

number of portraits of Biblical patriarchs, though these are now unfortunately badly deteriorated and heavily repainted. The entire decoration of the palace was carried out on the basis of a single iconographic program. This was probably suggested to the painter by the patriarch himself and by his theologians, including the vicar-general Francesco Florio, and centered on the history of the Chosen People, which indicated the way of salvation to the whole of humanity.

In the frescoes of the patriarchate of Udine – which mark the end of his juvenile production – Tiepolo arrived at a definition of the unmistakable style that was to distinguish his subsequent work. At this point it is easier to perceive his assimilation of Veronese's style. This assimilation had taken place gradually, first through a vague lightening of color, and only later through a deepening of his understanding of the more intimate secrets of Paolo's art, with the adoption of colored shadows in Palazzo Sandi and the use of complementary colors in Udine: in

other words the blend of color and light that constituted the principal characteristic of the painting of the great sixteenth-century artist. There were a lot of painters who went along with Tiepolo in this progressive absorption of Veronese's style, from Dorigny to Sebastiano Ricci, Pellegrini, and many others. But his capacity to take in that particular technique of painting, through the study of Paolo's works, was so great that Giambattista greatly surpassed the level reached by the other artists, to the point where he became, as was recognized even by his contemporaries, "another Veronese."

During the time he was painting the frescoes in Udine, between 1726 and 1729, he spent the winter months working on ten large canvases depicting scenes from Roman history. Up until 1870 these decorated the walls of the salon of Palazzo Dolfin in Venice, once again restored by Domenico Rossi. The clients for this new and grandiose undertaking were two brothers of the patriarch of Aquileia, Daniele III and Daniele IV, who wanted to celebrate, through prominent episodes from the history of the Roman republic, the devotion to their own country they had demonstrated in the diplomatic and military field. The canvases are now dispersed among the museums of St. Petersburg, Vienna, and New York: they reveal the maturity of technique now attained by

Tiepolo, who was able to imbue the scenes with a diffuse luminosity through his use of an unreal and extremely vivid light that brought out their colors.

Yet Tiepolo's activity in these years was certainly not limited to the commissions he received from the Dolfin family. In fact he painted numerous other works, often small in size but of exceptional interest. Among them were the ironic *Venus in the Mirror* formerly in the Gerli Collection in Milan, an irreverent paraphrase of Titian's models; the *Temptations of Saint Anthony* in Brera, with its exceptionally free approach to pictorial representation and refined colors; and *Apelles painting Campaspe's Portrait* in the Montreal Museum. This last painting has an autobiographical significance. Apelles was the mythical painter of antiquity who fell in love with Alexander the Great's lover, Campaspe, when asked to paint her. Alexander generously yielded the courtesan to him.

Giambattista chose to give Apelles his own features, while he portrayed Campaspe in the likeness of Cecilia Guardi, sister of the famous painters Antonio and Francesco, whom Tiepolo had secretly married in 1719. In fact the Guardi family – its head Domenico had died in 1717 – was in dire financial straits, and the decision to get married in secret was linked to Giambattista's fear that his mother would oppose the alliance, as the bride would bring no dowry. It is also worth noting that, contrary to the assumptions of some art historians, the marriage did not in any way signify a link between Tiepolo and his brothers-in-law, who carried out their activity under totally different circumstances.

Thus the painting is a homage to his young wife, and at the same time a testimony to the painter's proud awareness of his own ability, prompting him to give his own semblance to the most celebrated artist of antiquity.

16, 17. The Judgment of Solomon
Udine, Palazzo Patriarcale

18. The Triumph of Marius
545.5x324.5 cm
New York, Metropolitan Museum of Art

19. The Battle of Vercellae
431.8x375.9 cm
New York, Metropolitan Museum of Art

The Seventeen Thirties

By the end of the third decade of the century Tiepolo had built up a considerable reputation in the Veneto region. The next stage in his career came in 1730 when, perhaps through the intercession of the erudite Veronese Scipione Maffei, he was summoned to Milan. Here he painted five ceilings in Palazzo Archinto (the frescoes were destroyed in 1943) and, immediately afterward, worked in Palazzo Casati. Here he decorated the ceiling of the salon with what is usually considered an *Allegory of Magnanimity* (but more likely represents *The Apotheosis of Scipio*) and painted three scenes on the walls depicting *exempla virtutis* drawn from the life of Scipio himself. Unfortunately these frescoes are badly damaged and it is hard to interpret them. However in the best preserved of the scenes, representing *Scipio setting Free Masinissa*, the tranquillity of the narration and the quality of the color are still apparent.

On his return to Venice, Giambattista painted two important altarpieces in 1732. These were *The Education of the Virgin* for the church of Santa Maria della Consolazione, popularly known as the Chiesa della Fava, and the *Nativity* for that of San Zulian (now in St. Mark's basilica). Both of them show signs of a partial return to Piazzetta's manner in the vigorous plasticism of the figures and in the use of intense chiaroscuro. Yet the now typical features of Tiepolo's style can still be seen in the brilliance of the light, the rich and thickly laid-on paint, the Apollonian beauty of the faces of the large angels, and the way that the figures are linked together by the dynamics of their gestures and gazes. It was probably at this time that he painted the large frieze on canvas depicting *The Serpent of Brass* (or *The Scourge of Serpents*), which was originally placed under the choir of the church of Santi Cosma e Damiano on Giudecca and is now in the Gallerie dell'Accademia. After the work was removed at the beginning of the nineteenth century, the painting was left rolled up for a long time, which resulted in serious damage to the paint. In spite of this the canvas, over thirteen meters long, still displays the magnificent quality of the composition and Tiepolo's ex-

20. Abraham visited by the Angels
140x120 cm
Venice, Scuola Grande di San Rocco

21. Agar comforted by the Angel
140x120 cm
Venice, Scuola Grande di San Rocco

22. The Education of the Virgin
362x200 cm
Venice, church of Santa Maria della Consolazione

23

ceptional gift for coloring, with the silvery blue tones that have emerged from its recent restoration.

Between 1732 and 1733 Tiepolo was in Bergamo, where he worked on the decoration of the Colleoni Chapel in the cathedral: the three lunettes depicting *Scenes from the Life of the Baptist* are certainly to be considered one of his highest achievements of this period, owing to the delicate and yet incisive quality of the color. Apparent once again, in these works, is the influence of Veronese's models, although these are not imitated pedantically, but treated in a totally independent way, in a dimension all of his own.

In the summer of 1734 Giambattista went for the first time to Vicenza, where he had been summoned to fresco the grand staircase and the salon on the second floor of Count Nicolò Loschi's villa, which had just been restored by Francesco Muttoni. The allegorical figures in the decoration, represented with didactic clarity, are derived from Cesare Ripa's *Iconologia*. This was a popular iconographic repertory, first published in Rome at the end of the sixteenth century, on which Tiepolo frequently drew. What is surprising about these figures is the very clear quality of the color, which has grown limpid and bestows an almost classical elegance of form on the images.

The altarpiece in the parish church of Rovetta, in which Tiepolo embarks instead on a magnificent revival of the sixteenth-century manner, is roughly contemporary. In this case it is evident that the structure of the composition is derived from Titian's work, such

23. The Serpent of Brass
164x1356 cm
Venice, Gallerie
dell'Accademia

24. The Sermon of the
Baptist
350x300 cm
Bergamo, Colleoni Chapel

as the altarpiece representing the *Madonna in Glory and Child with Saints* that the artist from Cadore painted in 1538 for the Venetian church of San Nicolò della Lattuga, but which has been in the Vatican Museums since the nineteenth century. But the verve of the whole picture, in which all the personages are linked together by their gestures, is typical of the eighteenth century and confers a new vitality on the figures of the saints. The ceiling painted with *Zephyr and Flora* for a room in Palazzo Pesaro and subsequently transferred to the Museo del Settecento Veneziano in Ca' Rezzonico probably dates from the same period. Here the main figures are set on a dark cloud, but are bathed, like the beautiful flying putti that surround them, in a bright, Apollonian light.

Another genuine triumph of light is the small canvas depicting *Jupiter and Danaë*, bought while the paint was still fresh by Count Tessin on his visit to Venice in 1736 and now in the museum of Stockholm University. Here, with a wholly eighteenth-century sense of irony, evident for example in the squabble between Jupiter's symbol the eagle and the nymph's little dog, Tiepolo tackles the fable by Ovid that had been represented so many times by the great painters of the sixteenth century, offering an irreverent interpretation of the story. The same felicitous and sure brushstroke, which attains a synthesis of form and color of stupendous effect, is again to be found in the *Moses saved from the Waters* in Edinburgh Museum. It is a copy of a painting by Veronese that in the early eighteenth century was in the Grimani Collection

25. The Beheading of the Baptist
350x300 cm
Bergamo, Colleoni Chapel

26. Magnanimity bestowing her Gifts
230x180 cm
Biron (Vicenza), Villa Loschi Zileri dal Verme

27. Virtue crowning Honor
230x180 cm
Biron (Vicenza), Villa Loschi Zileri dal Verme

28. Marital Concord
230x180 cm
Biron (Vicenza), Villa Loschi Zileri dal Verme

29. Humility driving out Pride (page 27)
230x180 cm
Biron (Vicenza), Villa Loschi Zileri dal Verme

in Venice and is now in the Dresden Museum. The canvas in Edinburgh, commissioned by the Cornaro family, has been badly mutilated: probably to remedy the fact that the Pharaoh's daughter was not in the middle of the painting, a large piece was cut off on the right-hand side. Containing the figure of a *Halberdier*, it is now in a private collection in Turin.

The closing years of the fourth decade saw Tiepolo again working for clients from outside Venice. In 1737 he returned to Milan, where he had been called by Cardinal Erba Odescalchi to paint some frescoes in the basilica of Sant'Ambrogio. From 1737 to 1738 he produced three altarpieces for Patriarch Dolfin in Udine, one for the church of Santa Maria Maddalena and the other two for the cathedral. Before the end of 1739 he painted the large altarpiece depicting *Pope Saint Clement worshipping the Trinity* for the high altar of Notre Dame in the Nymphenburg, now in Munich's Alte Pinakothek. The picture is characterized by the swirling dynamism of the composition and the splendid orchestration of colors centering on the strong contrast between the areas in shadow and the ones in the light. A beautiful study for it was acquired by the National Gallery in London in 1957: it differs substantially from the larger version in the structure of the composition and in the arrangement of the figures. This is a recurrent feature of the sketches that Tiepolo habitually painted as a preparation for his large-scale works. Their function, evidently, was to provide the client with a preview in miniature of the larger work, so that he could inform the painter of any alterations that he wished to be made, whether to

30, 32. The Triumph of Zephyr and Flora
395x225 cm
Venice, Ca'Rezzonico

31. Jupiter and Danaë
41x53 cm
Stockholm, Universitet Konsthistoriska Institutionen

*33. Madonna in Glory
with Apostles and Saints
378x234 cm
Rovetta (Bergamo),
church of Ognissanti*

the style, the iconography, or just the coloring, right from the start. In this case the client must have found the scene represented in the sketch too spread out and the figures too far apart: hence the considerable differences to be found in the altarpiece, where the monumental figures of the canonized pope and the Trinity have been shifted into the foreground and made much more conspicuous.

There can be no doubt that his most important undertaking at the end of the fourth decade was the fresco decoration of the new church of the Gesuati, designed by Giorgio Massari and built between 1726 and 1735. Tiepolo was at work on the frescoes on the ceiling of the nave, presbytery, and chancel from 1737 to 1739. Especially significant is the central panel of the ceiling of the nave, depicting *The Institution of the Rosary*. This represents a genuine homage to Veronese, and in particular to his *Assumption of the Virgin* which in the eighteenth century was still in its original location, the nearby church of the Umiltà (subsequently Veronese's ceiling was removed and transferred to the chapel of the Rosary in Santi Giovanni e Paolo).

In preparation for this fresco Giambattista presented his clients with three different sketches: evidently the Dominicans of the monastery of the Gesuati were not completely satisfied with the scene he had devised and had suggested numerous modifications. These were concerned in particular with certain iconographic aspects that were of undoubted importance if the message conveyed by the frescoes was to be clear to the faithful: the

34. Pope Saint Clement worshipping the Trinity (sketch)
69.2x55.2 cm
London, National Gallery

35. The Institution of the Rosary
1200x450 cm
Venice, church of the Gesuati

36. The Road to Calvary
450x517 cm
Venice, church of Sant'Alvise

glorification of the Order as expressed through the Virgin's placing of the Rosary in the hands of its holy founder and, at the same time, the confirmation of the Order's close links with Venice, symbolized by the presence in the fresco of the current doge, Alvise Pisani, and the patriarch, Francesco Antonio Correr.

What stands out in this and the other frescoes in the nave is the light and luminous, almost iridescent shades of color, typical of Tiepolo's palette. The narration of the events is simple and calm and makes a decisive contribution to the atmosphere of refined decoration that characterizes the whole of the interior of Massari's church, an authentic gem of sophisticated Venetian rococo. Everything is dominated by the light, an artificial light of Apollonian and in some ways unique splendor, that bathes the figures and heightens their role.

Contemporaneously with his decoration of the Gesuati, he painted the three large canvases depicting

resentations of fanciful and magical subjects and achieves an abstract sense of the fantastic.

In 1740 Giambattista went back to Milan for the last time. He had been summoned by Marchese Giorgio Clerici to decorate the ceiling of the gallery in his palace, in preparation for his marriage to Fulvia Visconti the following year. Tiepolo painted *The Course of the Chariot of the Sun*, tackling for the first time a theme that he was to repeat on numerous other occasions. Apollo's chariot drawn by four pawing white steeds is set in the middle of the ceiling. A few other deities are moving through the sky, illuminated by the strong light of dawn. But in the groups arranged on the molding and amidst the painted architecture Giambattista gives free rein to his incomparable imagination. The result is a genuine phantasmagoria of figures portrayed in the most disparate positions, in groups or isolation, that represent the gods of Olympus, the four parts of the known world at that time, the sea, rivers, and still others.

The fresco in Palazzo Clerici constitutes another turning point in the development of Tiepolo's artistic personality: here Giambattista shows that he is now capable of dominating any space whatsoever, even such a difficult one as the extremely long, narrow and fairly low gallery, through the force of his imagination and the superb quality of his color, which is transparent, sumptuous, and yet classically detached.

The conclusion of the work on the fresco in Palazzo Clerici – even though it was still praised in the following century as "the most marvelous work, above all for its handling of light" to have been painted in Milan during the eighteenth century – coincided with an abrupt interruption of Tiepolo's relations with the local nobility. The reason for this lay in the new cultural climate that emerged in Milan after Maria Theresa's ascent of the imperial throne, an event that took place in that same year of 1740: from that moment on the city became one of the main centers of the Enlightenment in Italy and this more realistic climate was no longer favorable to Tiepolo's art, with its Apollonian triumphs and celebration of the glories and deeds of his clients. For the same reason Tiepolo, the prince of *ancien régime* painters, never went to Enlightenment France, even though numerous Venetian rococo artists, such as Giovanni Antonio Pellegrini, Sebastiano Ricci, and Rosalba Carriera, had achieved great success there in the first two decades of the century, or to England, the leading example of an enlightened monarchy.

Scenes from the Passion of Christ that were hung in the church of Sant'Alvise in Venice by the end of 1740. In these exceptional masterpieces the atmosphere is decidedly more dramatic. For once, the source of Tiepolo's inspiration is not Paolo Veronese but the works of Tintoretto and Titian. Giambattista shows a thorough familiarity with the latter's *Christ Crowned with Thorns*, which in the eighteenth century was still in its original location, the church of Santa Maria delle Grazie in Milan, but is now in the Louvre. However the canvases in Sant'Alvise also reveal a new interest in the works of Rembrandt, as can be seen from the presence, especially in the *Road to Calvary*, of bearded and prophetic old men who seem to have been derived from the engravings of the Dutch master.

Rembrandt's engravings also exercised a great influence on Giambattista in the series of etchings of *Caprices* that he made in the 1730s, and in the one of *Jests* in the following decade. These are perhaps the most significant engravings to have been produced in Venice in the eighteenth century. The poetic handling of light goes well beyond what was usual in such rep-

*37, 38. The Course of the Chariot of the Sun, details
Milan, Palazzo Clerici*

The Years of Maturity

Returning to Venice at the end of 1740, Giambattista painted the enormous altarpieces for the parish church of Verolanuova and devoted himself in particular to the decoration of public and private premises. In June 1743 he installed the eight lateral canvases of the ceiling of the chapterhouse of the Scuola Grande dei Carmini, dominated by the sumptuous, sensual beauty of the figures of the Virtues. At the same time he painted the fresco in the salon of Palazzo Pisani Moretta celebrating the glories of Admiral Vettor Pisani, victor over the Genoese in the War of Chioggia and ancestor of Chiara Pisani, the work's client. The illustrious commander, accompanied by Venus, ascends Olympus to be presented to Jupiter, father of the gods, and Mars, god of war. Naturally, Neptune, king of the sea, looks on. *The Portrait of Antonio Riccobono* in the Accademia dei Concordi at Rovigo dates from the same year. Riccobono was a sixteenth-century writer from that city and Giambattista evidently based his likeness on a contemporary source. Yet he succeeded in imparting an exceptional vitality to the figure, almost as if the portrait had been painted from life. The paint itself is rich, frayed, and laid on with incredible speed, in broad and confident brushstrokes. It does not seem excessive to claim that Tiepolo took his inspiration here from the portraits of Titian's late period, so evident are the parallels with the *Portrait of Jacopo*

Strada in the Kunsthistorisches Museum of Vienna. The figure of the sixteenth-century antiquarian could almost be superimposed on that of Riccobono, even though they are facing in opposite directions. A similar luminous quality can be seen in an unusual and moving devotional image now in the Moss Collection in New York. According to an old inscription on the back of the canvas, it represents the *Blessed Laduina*.

It was at this time that he painted his first works for the court in Dresden, a commission he received through the good offices of Count Francesco Algarotti, who acted as a go-between and art consultant to the elector of Saxony and king of Poland, Augustus III. They included

39. The Sacrifice of Melchizedec
1000x525 cm
Verolanuova (Brescia), parish church

40. The Collection of Manna
1000x525 cm
Verolanuova (Brescia), parish church

41. Apotheosis of Admiral Vettor Pisani
Venice, Palazzo Pisani Moretta

the *Banquet of Antony and Cleopatra*, now in Melbourne, and for which a study exists in the luminous sketch now in the Musée Cognacq-Jay in Paris. It constitutes the first version of a subject that was to find its highest expression in the frescoes of the salon of Palazzo Labia. In addition there were two extremely elegant canvases of small size depicting *Maecenas presenting the Arts to Augustus* (now in the Hermitage in St. Petersburg) and *The Triumph of Flora* (now in the M.H. de Young Memorial Museum in San Francisco). These last, sent in 1744 to Augustus's powerful minister and adviser, Count Bruhl, are characterized by the light quality of the paint and their vibrant luminosity.

Algarotti, a Venetian pupil of the architectural theoretician Carlo Lodoli, was a fine connoisseur of art and an aggressive collector who frequented the most progressive salons in Europe and popularized Newton's theories on light and color in Venice. He played a role of some significance in the development of Tiepolo's career, above and beyond the important and lucrative commissions he obtained for the artist. In fact it was through Algarotti that Giambattista came into contact with a new world, the refined and classical style of French painting. And some echo of this new influence is to be found in the works of this period: not only in the two

42. The Blessed Laduina
65x48 cm
Riverdale on Hudson (New York),
Stanley Moss Collection

aforementioned pictures for Bruhl, but also in several small canvases of mythological subjects, such as the *Diana and Actaeon* in a private collection in Zurich, which used to belong to Algarotti himself, the *Apollo and the Muses* in the Crane Collection in New York, and the *Apollo and Daphne* in the Louvre, where the figures are set in vast landscapes.

Between 1743 and 1744 Tiepolo was at Montecchio Maggiore, near Vicenza, working on the decoration of the villa built by Giorgio Massari for the jurist Carlo Cordellina, where he painted a series of frescoes in the salon. In the central panel of the ceiling, surrounded by a set of six allegorical figures in monochrome, Giambattista painted *The Triumph of Virtue and Nobility over Ignorance*, while the walls were decorated with two large scenes representing *Darius's Family before Alexander* and the *Restraint of Scipio*. In the first of these two frescoes – whose subjects are intended as *exempla virtutis* – the derivation from Veronese is particularly evident, given that Tiepolo used as his model Paolo's painting of

the same subject. He must have seen the picture not long before in Palazzo Pisani Moretta, for it was not until the nineteenth century that it found its way to England (where it is now in the National Gallery in London).

Completing this commission in 1744, Giambattista returned to Venice, where he worked, again in collaboration with Mengozzi Colonna, on the decoration of two rooms on the *piano nobile* of Palazzo Barbarigo at Santa Maria del Giglio. The most notable of this series is the ceiling depicting *The Triumph of Virtue and Nobility over Ignorance*, which was transferred to the Museo del Settecento Veneziano in Ca' Rezzonico in 1936. It is undoubtedly the best of Giambattista's many versions of this theme, which was much to the liking of his noble clients because of its obvious self-congratulatory significance.

This was an extremely busy period in Giambattista's career, which saw him engaged in a large number of commissions of exceptional importance. For a Venetian palace that has yet to be identified – but in any case not the home of the man who was to become the last doge of

43. Portrait of Antonio Riccobono
102x90 cm
Rovigo, Accademia dei Concordi

44. *Apollo and Daphne*
96x79 cm
Paris, Louvre

45. Rinaldo and the Magus of Ascalon
186.9x214.7 cm
Chicago, Art Institute

Venice, Ludovico Manin, as has been supposed – he painted the series of eight canvases whose subjects were derived from Torquato Tasso's *Jerusalem Delivered*. Now equally divided between the Chicago Museum and the National Gallery in London, they were probably accompanied, in their original location, by three ornamental panels over doors with figures of male and female satyrs (two of which are now in the Norton Simon Foundation of Pasadena, while the third is in Rome's Galleria Nazionale d'Arte Antica). The paintings now in London and Chicago represent the first occasion on which the painter used images derived from a literary poem for the decoration of a patrician residence, rather than from the usual repertory of myths and allegories. What is most significant here is the setting chosen for the events, Arcadian landscapes of a rather disturbing character, and certainly extraneous to the spirit of the epic poem, as if Tasso had been reinterpreted through the eyes of a Metastasio.

In the summer of 1745 he decorated the ceiling of the nave of the Venetian church of the Scalzi with the large fresco of *The Transport of the Holy House of Loreto*, which was to be destroyed by an Austrian incendiary bomb in 1915. All that is left of it – apart from the vaulting cells and a few parts of the painted molding that were saved after the bombing and are now in the Gallerie dell'Accademia in Venice, offering an eloquent testimony to the limpid symphony of pale shades of color that characterized the whole work – are two preparatory studies, which reveal the process of the work's conception. The older of the two – the one in the same Venetian galleries – shows the house on the right, borne aloft by a group of angels; its presence is balanced, on the left, by a second group of angels playing music. The second one, which was recently acquired by the Paul Getty Museum in Malibu from the British Rail Pension Fund, is a reworking of it. The painter, probably on the instruction of the clients – the Carmelite monks who lived in the monastery adjoining the majestic church – has radically altered the layout of the scene, moving the house to the left and adding numerous groups of figures, whose forms are similar to the ones that would eventually appear in the fresco. In September of the same year Giambattista delivered to Bergamo Cathedral the large altarpiece depicting the *Martyrdom of Saint John of Rochester*. This had been commissioned from him in 1743, but its execution had been delayed for two years as a consequence of the huge number of engagements that he had taken on in the meantime. Critics have seen some of the minor figures in the background, more carefully drawn and realistic in appearance, as the work of Giambattista's eldest son, Giandomenico, born in 1727. From around this time he became his father's most diligent and faithful collaborator, accompanying him constantly on his work trips and assisting him in all major decorative undertakings. There are many independent works by Giandomenico, which show him to be a very different painter from his father, in culture, interests, character, and technique. Yet when he collaborated with Giambattista he was able to imitate his style perfectly, so that it is not easy to distinguish their work. This demonstrates just how strict a control the head of the studio exercised over his assistants.

Tiepolo's intervention in Palazzo Labia, owned by one of the wealthiest of the new noble Venetian families, can reasonably be dated to 1746-47. It consisted largely of the decoration of the ballroom, which covered the entire surface of the ceiling and walls. On the ceiling, inside a large central oculus and against the dazzling blue of the sky, appears Bellerophon mounted on the white winged horse Pegasus, soaring toward Glory and Eternity. On the walls, surrounded by painted architecture filled with allegorical and mythological figures, are set the two main scenes, depicting *The Meeting of Antony and Cleopatra* and their *Banquet*. The whole intervention is a splendid testimony to Tiepolo's unsurpassed gift for decoration: he responded to the magnificence of the architectural framework painted by Gerolamo Mengozzi Colonna, capable of creating infinite though illusory spaces that extend beyond the real walls, by producing the most fascinating theatrical scenes that he had ever painted. The observer cannot but feel that Antony and Cleopatra, along with their retinue of servants, sorcerers, and soldiers, are about to descend from the wharf by the painted flight of steps and seat themselves at the stately repast laid out on the opposite wall, beneath a portico. In Palazzo Labia history is turned into reality: but, in a wholly eighteenth-century spirit, the events are narrated in a frivolous and witty manner, even with a touch of malice at times. Everything is dominated by Tiepolo's extraordinary talent for coloring, yielding a triumph of delicate and luminous tints that are still sufficiently clear in spite of the damage suffered by the frescoes. At the same time they reveal his exceptional gift for narrative, expressed in this case through a fast paced rhythm, of great vitality.

The frescoes in the adjoining Sala degli Specchi are of similar quality. The ceiling is decorated with a *Triumph of Zephyr and Flora* in which the colors are wonderfully bright and the figures sparkle with life.

It was not until he had completed the decoration of Palazzo Labia that Tiepolo consigned the central panel of the ceiling of the chapterhouse in the Scuola dei Carmini, representing the *Virgin giving the Scapular to Saint Simon Stock*. He also delivered to the church of the Gesuati the altarpiece depicting *Three Dominican Saints* that had been commissioned from him at the end of 1739, when he had finished work on the series of frescoes for that church which have already been mentioned. The altarpiece, characterized by the crystalline quality of its

46. *The Transport of the Holy House of Loreto (sketch)*
124x85 cm
Venice, Gallerie dell'Accademia

47. *Bellerophon soaring toward Glory and Eternity*
diam. 600 cm
Venice, Palazzo Labia

48. *The Meeting of Antony and Cleopatra (page 44)*
650x300 cm
Venice, Palazzo Labia

49. *The Banquet of Antony and Cleopatra (page 45)*
650x300 cm
Venice, Palazzo Labia

50, 52. *The Banquet of Antony and Cleopatra, details*
Venice, Palazzo Labia

51, 53. *The Meeting of Antony and Cleopatra, details*
Venice, Palazzo Labia

54. *The Winds, detail*
Venice, Palazzo Labia

55. The Communion of Saint Lucy
222x101 cm
Venice, church of the Santi Apostoli

56. The Virgin giving the Scapular
to Saint Simon Stock
533x432 cm
Venice, Scuola Grande dei Carmini

57. Three Dominican Saints
340x168 cm
Venice, church of the Gesuati

color, the elegant monumentality of its composition, and the perfect, almost classical beauty of the saints' faces, is certainly one of his greatest achievements in the field of religious painting. Quite similar features are to be found in the *Communion of Saint Lucy*. Painted around the same time as an ornament for the sixteenth-century chapel of the noble Cornaro family in the church of Santi Apostoli, it presents a radiant symphony of colors.

Other works of particular interest date from around 1750. Among these it is worth mentioning at least the *Portrait of a Dolfin as Procurator and Capitano da Mar* (probably the same Daniele IV who had been one of the clients for the scenes from Roman history that he had painted between 1726 and 1729 for the salon of the family's palace at San Pantalon). Now in the Fondazione Querini Stampalia in Venice, it is one of the very few portraits of noblemen painted by Tiepolo. In addition, there were the canvases he painted for one of the rooms in Palazzo Barbaro. This group includes the ceiling depicting the *Glorification of the Family*, now in New York's Metropolitan Museum, and four ornamental panels set

above doors representing emblematic episodes from the lives of famous women of antiquity. Now dispersed among several different collections, they are in a magnificent revival of the sixteenth-century style and wonderfully balanced from the point of view of composition.

The exceptional *Saint James the Greater*, painted for the Spanish ambassador in London, Ricardo Wall, and now in the Budapest Museum, dates from the same year. The effect of the painting is based on the strong chromatic contrast between the warrior saint's white horse in the foreground and the blue of the sky in the background. The dramatic figures of horsemen engaged in a furious skirmish that appear in the background also provide a contrast to the resolute calm of the main figure, whose face, resplendent with light, is set off by the red standard that flies above. The large canvas depicting *The Patron Saints of the Crotta Family* and again of a classical splendor in the sixteenth-century manner, which is now in Frankfurt's Städelsches Kunstinstitut, should be considered contemporary.

58. *Portrait of a Dolfin as Procurator and Capitano da Mar*
235x158 cm
Venice, Fondazione Querini Stampalia

59. *Glorification of the Barbaro Family*
253.8x466.8 cm
New York, Metropolitan Museum of Art

60. *Saint James the Greater*
317x163 cm
Budapest, Szépművészeti Museum

The Würzburg Residenz and the Frescoes in Villa Valmarana

In December 1750 Giambattista, accompanied by his sons Giandomenico and Lorenzo, went to Würzburg. He had been summoned there by Prince Bishop Karl Philipp von Greiffenklau to fresco the large dining room of the Residence, which only later came to be known as the Kaisersaal. Within the framework of the ceiling's fanciful decoration of white and gold stuccoes designed by the Lombard Antonio Bossi, Tiepolo painted *Apollo leading Beatrice of Burgundy to the Genius of the German Nation*. Beatrice was shortly to be married to Frederick Barbarossa. Immediately afterward he set to work on the wall scenes, where he painted *The Marriage of Barbarossa* and *The Investiture of Bishop Harold as Duke of Franconia*, which bears the date 1752, the year he completed work on the room. The client's satisfaction is demonstrated by the fact that he straightaway entrusted Giambattista with the task of painting the fresco on the majestic vault of the grand staircase. Here the artist depicted *Mount Olympus and the Four Continents*, based in part on the similar subject he had painted in the gallery of Palazzo Clerici in 1740. It appears that the work on this second ceiling was concluded by November 1753, when Giambattista set off to return to Venice.

The three frescoes in the dining room should be considered genuine masterpieces for the richness of the paint, laid on in broad areas of color balanced between the sumptuous drapery of the figures' clothes and the luminous clarity of the blue skies. Shades of white and silver, deep blue, red, and purple create a symphony of solemn proportions, that displays all the limpid delicacy of the rococo. Even the molding of white and gold now seems absolutely familiar to Tiepolo, who makes unconstrained use of it to create the effects of atmospheric transparency that so clearly differentiate his extremely

61, 62. Apollo leading Beatrice of Burgundy to the Genius of the German Nation
900x1800 cm
Würzburg, Residenz, Kaisersaal

63. The Marriage of Barbarossa and Beatrice of Burgundy
400x500 cm. Würzburg, Residenz, Kaisersaal

64. The Investiture of Bishop Harold as Duke of Franconia
400x500 cm. Würzburg, Residenz, Kaisersaal

65, 66. The Four Parts of the World, detail of Africa
Würzburg, Residenz, staircase

67. *The Four Parts of the World, detail of America*
Würzburg, Residenz, staircase

68. *The Four Parts of the World, detail of Europe*
Würzburg, Residenz, staircase

69. *The Four Parts of the World, detail of Asia*
Würzburg, Residenz, staircase

elegant decorative style from that of the late baroque schools that preceded him and that were still strong in the German-speaking countries.

Even in the representation of the subjects – over which he had no choice – his independence is clearly apparent. In fact the two scenes of the *Marriage* and *Investiture* were part of an earlier plan of decoration for the Residence drawn up in 1735 by the Jesuit fathers Seyfried and Gilbert. However this scheme for the glorification of the local prince bishops placed the two episodes among the paintings of the grand staircase, along with four other historical scenes. Likewise, a plan produced in 1742 envisaged five historical scenes to be painted on the ceiling of the staircase, but they did not include the two scenes painted by Tiepolo in the dining room.

In the last program, which was the one sent to Tiepolo in Venice in 1750, the two scenes are located in the future Kaisersaal. Undoubtedly this final solution – evidently the result of an extremely complicated process – met with the painter's approval. The two wall scenes, with their frontal presentation as if they were sumptuous stage sets, are well suited to his "Veronesian" vision, already tried out in previous years. The central oval, on the other hand, which to some extent also echoes the *Olympus* in Palazzo Clerici with the inclusion of Apollo's chariot drawn by four fiery white steeds, appears to be entirely the fruit of Tiepolo's own imagination. And yet the adroit structure of the fresco's composition, whose alternation of solids and voids appears to recapitulate the undulating surface of the room's walls, and the variety and liveliness of the stuccoes and the segmented vault, opening up illusionistically here and there to let in a cascade of clouds and winged figures, is perfectly integrated with the setting.

Giambattista's marvelous and unsurpassable creative imagination is even more forcefully revealed in the fresco on the ceiling of the staircase: a complex but unitary representation centering on the triumphant figure of Apollo, god of Light, which opens onto a bright and

During his stay in Würzburg, Tiepolo also painted various religious pictures on canvas. One of them was the *Adoration of the Magi* for the Benedictine church at Schwarzach, now in Munich's Alte Pinakothek, inspired by Paolo Veronese's altarpiece of the same subject in Santa Corona in Venice. It is distinguished by the extraordinary touch of the blaze of silvery blue light that bathes the main figures of the Virgin and Child, rendered in very pale, almost pastel shades of color.

On his return to Venice, Tiepolo resumed his frantic pace of work. His main undertaking of this period was the decoration of the new church of the Pietà, designed by Giorgio Massari as a large music room for the concerts of the institute's celebrated "little girls." The main fresco on the vault of the nave, painted in 1754, depicts *The Coronation of the Blessed Virgin*: numerous angels playing instruments and choristers participate in the event, to underline the connection between the sacredness of the place and the music that was performed there. A summary sketch for this work is known as well. Recently acquired by the Kimbell Art Museum in Fort Worth, it presents numerous differences from the final version.

In 1757 Tiepolo returned for the last time to Vicenza. He had been called there by Count Giustino Valmarana, a cultivated man of letters and lover of the theater who must have personally chosen the subjects for the frescoes to decorate the rooms of the house and guest quarters that made up his villa. Giambattista took charge of decorating the house, delegating the paintings in the guest quarters to his son Giandomenico, with the exception of the ceiling of the room called the Sala dell'Olimpo.

In the house Tiepolo returned to literary themes, taking his inspiration from the works of great poets of antiquity (Homer and Virgil) and the Renaissance (Ariosto and Tasso). The decoration of the central hall and the four rooms at the sides took on a more intimate, less grandiloquent tone, partly because of the limited size of the rooms. Its refined elegance is enhanced by the moldings that enclose the scenes, designed by Mengozzi Colonna in different forms for each room. The narration of events is obviously influenced by the client's fascination with the theater: the heroes and gods of the classical poems, like the knights and damsels of the Renaissance ones, become actors in a melodramatic play centering on the representation of feelings.

transparent sky dotted with celestial apparitions. On the molding, departing from the various programs drawn up for the decoration of this space, Tiepolo painted representations of the *Four Parts of the World*. The dozens of different figures located in the section reserved for Europe include the authors of this superb masterpiece: the architect Balthasar Neumann, who died on August 19, 1753, while Giambattista was still at work up on the scaffolding, portrayed in the guise of an artillery colonel; the designer of the stucco decoration, Antonio Bossi; the painter Franz Ignaz Roth, Tiepolo's collaborator; and finally Giambattista and, next to him, his son Giandomenico. Higher up, from a gilded oval supported by Fame and crowned by the Virgin, the client looks on. The whole scene is steeped in an Apollonian, dazzling light, which renders the colors clear and transparent.

70. The Coronation of the Blessed Virgin
1320x700 cm
Venice, church of the Pietà

71. The Adoration of the Magi
405x211 cm
Munich, Alte Pinakothek

72. *The Sacrifice
of Iphigenia
350x700 cm
Vicenza,
Villa Valmarana*

73. Minerva keeping Achilles
from killing Agamemnon
300x300 cm
Vicenza, Villa Valmarana

74. Soldiers between columns
350x115 cm
Vicenza, Villa Valmarana

75. *Angelica taking Leave of Medoro, detail*
Vicenza, Villa Valmarana

76. *Angelica cutting Medoro's Name into*
a Tree Trunk
250x160 cm
Vicenza, Villa Valmarana

77. *Aeneas introducing Cupid dressed*
as Ascanius to Dido (page 66)
230x240 cm
Vicenza, Villa Valmarana

78. *Rinaldo abandoning Armida (page 66)*
220x310 cm
Vicenza, Villa Valmarana

66

The Last Venetian Works and his Departure for Spain

With the decoration for Count Valmarana concluded in the fall, Tiepolo went back to Venice. Here, in Palazzo Rezzonico, he painted two ceilings in the rooms intended for the newly-wed Ludovico Rezzonico and Faustina Savorgnan with his customary, lightning speed. The two frescoes return to eulogistic themes that he had used previously: in the first scene Apollo's chariot and four white and mettlesome horses once again fly toward the future fortunes of the young couple; in the second Merit ascends to the temple of immortal Glory, accompanied by Nobility and Virtue and preceded by Fame sounding her trumpet. Yet once again Tiepolo's genius succeeds in creating images of unsurpassable power, perfect and crystalline in form and characterized by colors that grow brighter under the effect of the dazzling light.

The work in Ca' Rezzonico was the last major decoration carried out by Giambattista in Venice. From then on, in fact, Tiepolo painted only a few works on can-

79. Nobility and Virtue leading Merit to the Temple of Glory
1000x600 cm
Venice, Ca'Rezzonico

80. Neptune offering Gifts to Venice
135x275 cm
Venice, Doge's Palace

vas for his own city. These included the neo-Verone-sian painting in the sixteenth-century manner, *Neptune offering Gifts to Venice*, one of the very few pictures painted for the Doge's Palace during the eighteenth century. It is very similar in style, to the point where it may be considered contemporary, to the canvas depicting *Time unveiling Truth* in Boston's Museum of Fine Arts and to the ceiling representing *Venus entrusting a Son to Time*, acquired by the National Gallery in London in 1961. In the meantime, during the years which preceded his departure for Madrid, he resumed his wanderings. In 1759 he visited Udine for the last

time, where he decorated the oratory of the Purità. In the same year he painted an altarpiece for Este Cathedral representing *Saint Thecla interceding for the Liberation of the City from Plague*. There is a wonderful study for this in New York's Metropolitan Museum, painted with the rapidity that characterizes the small canvases of the latter part of his career.

At the same time he worked for Tsarina Helena Petrovna, painting, among other things, a series of "half-length figures of women from imagination than which no finer and more perfect things can be seen," as his contemporary Francesco Maria Tassi described them. Among them was the wonderful *Young Woman with a Parrot* in the Ashmolean Museum in Oxford, yet another return to the models of the cinquecento and a painting of exceptional quality. It must have been during the same period

68

of time that he painted the pair of refined ornamental panels with mythological figures (*Venus and Vulcan, Apollo and Daphne*). At the end of the century they were still together in a Viennese collection but have now been split up between the Johnson Collection in Philadelphia and the National Gallery in Washington.

In 1760 Giambattista accepted a commission from the Pisani family to fresco a ceiling in the main salon of their villa at Stra, celebrating the glories of the extremely powerful family and, through them, of Venice itself. In a letter to his friend Algarotti, the painter declared that it would be a "not so trifling work that will keep me occupied for three or four years." But this turned out to be an optimistic prediction: in fact he found that he had to paint the large ceiling as quickly as possible (and, at the same time, the one depicting the *Triumph of*

Hercules in Palazzo Canossa in Verona, all but destroyed by a bombing raid in 1945), since King Charles III of Spain required his presence in Madrid, even exerting pressure on the government of the Serenissima through his ambassador in Venice. And Giambattista accepted the prestigious invitation: having completed the Pisani's *Triumph*, in which the clients themselves are shown taken up into heaven among the Olympians, and left to others the task of finishing the decoration of the walls of the salon in the villa at Stra, he set off for Madrid on March 31, 1762, accompanied by his sons Giandomenico and Lorenzo. He arrived there, after a perilous journey, on June 4.

There has been much debate over the reasons why the painter, now aged sixty-six, made the undoubtedly traumatic choice to leave his native city and face the dangers

porter of the *Nuova Veneta Gazzetta* in the famous interview he gave in March 1762. And by now it was not easy to meet "Noble Lords, and rich ones" in Venice who were disposed to invest their own money in enormous and amazing decorative projects that were out of fashion.

The task assigned to him by Charles III was the decoration of the immense ceiling of the Throne Room in the Royal Palace, which had just been rebuilt by Sacchetti to plans drawn up by Filippo Juvarra. On it Giambattista painted *The Glory of Spain*, in which the inexhaustible power of his decorative imagination is once again revealed in full, allowing him to produce – despite the reutilization of schemes he had already adopted in the past – a picture of the highest quality. Thus the fresco can be seen as a brilliant recapitulation of his earlier decorations, but also as further proof of Giambattista's superb mastery of perspective and of the orchestration of color, so that the work as a whole is one of absolute originality.

Certainly, given the now advanced age of the painter, afflicted even during his last years in Venice by a "most insolent gout" that had caused him to delay starting on the salon in Villa Pisani, much of the work on the fresco in the Throne Room was carried out by his sons. And yet it displays a complete homogeneity of style, owing to the ability of both Giandomenico and Lorenzo to mimic – here, as on all the other occasions they collaborated with Giambattista – their father's style, perfectly translating his desire for perfection of form and wonderfully luminous coloring.

With *The Glory of Spain* completed in 1764, Tiepolo was commissioned to decorate the ceilings of two more rooms in the palace: the Hall of the Halberdiers and the Antechamber of the Queen. Here Giambattista painted the scenes of the *Apotheosis of Aeneas* and the *Triumph of the Spanish Monarchy*, which have similar qualities to those of his first fresco in Madrid.

Once he had finished this demanding undertaking in 1766, Giambattista took the painful decision not to return home and informed Charles III that he was prepared to stay in Madrid and continue working for the Spanish court. The following year he was given the job of painting altarpieces for the seven altars of the royal church at Aranjuez, a task that he completed within the short space of two years. But Giambattista never had the chance to see the canvases installed: it was only after his death, in fact, that the paintings were placed on the altars for a brief period, only to be removed and replaced by pictures by the neoclassical artists Mengs, Maella, and Bayeu, in 1775. Tiepolo's altarpieces have been dispersed among a variety of collections and in some cases even broken up. Nevertheless they constitute an excellent example of his incisive coloring, some-

of a long journey and the difficulties of an unknown environment. Certainly one powerful motivation may have been the desire to carry out another grandiose decorative assignment in the palace of one of the oldest and most prestigious monarchies of Europe. But Tiepolo's decision must also have been influenced by the knowledge that his art, with its emphasis on Apollonian triumphs, on glorification of his clients' virtues, was now in conflict with the new culture that was beginning to take root even around the lagoon, and appeared out of date. It is no coincidence, in fact, that since the end of 1757 the celebrated "new Veronese" had not been receiving the most prestigious commissions in Venice, but only on the mainland. "Painters have to be able to succeed in major works, that is in the ones that might be pleasing to Noble Lords, and rich ones, for these make the fortune of Professors, and not other people, who cannot buy Pictures of much value," Giambattista would declare to the re-

81. Time unveiling Truth
231x167 cm
Boston, Museum of Fine Arts

82. Venus entrusting a Son to Time
292x190.5 cm
London, National Gallery

what simplified here but still very impressive. The paintings for Aranjuez – for which he produced a series of beautiful studies: the ones known to have survived are owned by Count Seilern and on show at the Courtauld Institute in London – are characterized by an unprecedented accentuation of realism and pathos: in the vegetable garden of the presbytery, St. Paschal Baylon has a vision of an angel bringing him the Holy Sacrament and abandons his work, dropping the hoe on the ground; an enfeebled St. Francis receives the stigmata – lying on his humble litter; St. Peter of Alcántara, surrounded by books in his study, has a vision of the dove of the Holy Spirit; the Madonna of splendid classical beauty in the *Immaculate Conception* in the Prado, ringed by lively flying putti, is portrayed trampling on the serpent tempter. However limited, these innovations that now appeared in Giambattista's pictorial language are still surprising. The only credible explanation is that the aging painter was trying to adapt his modes of expression as far as possible to the new neoclassical aesthetics that were now in vogue even at the Spanish court. The main supporter

of the new style was the king's powerful confessor and patron of Mengs, the Franciscan Joaquin de Electa. Leaving aside the unsubstantiated and probably fanciful stories told by many critics of the hostility encountered by Giambattista during the last years of his life in Spain, the painter must have been quite aware of the change in his clients' expectations and tried to adapt to them.

Another fruit of this attempt was a series of small paintings of religious subjects, characterized by very light colors and a trembling hand: *The Flight into Egypt by Boat* in the Museu de Arte Antigua in Lisbon, in which two angels with widespread wings steer the vessel on which the Holy Family has taken ship; *The Rest on the*

*83. Saint Thecla interceding for the Liberation of the City of Este from Plague, detail
Este, cathedral*

*84. Young Woman with a Parrot
70x52 cm
Oxford, Ashmolean Museum*

Flight into Egypt, now in Stuttgart, where the tiny figures are almost lost in the bleak landscape with its rugged mountains and a tall Maritime pine clambering up the barren rocks; or again the beautiful *Deposition* in Lisbon, which seems to convey the touching resignation of the old artist, now close to death. And yet he still had the strength to accept, at the end of 1769, another important commission: that of frescoing the vault of the collegiate church of Sant'Ildefonso at La Granja. But he was only able to paint the preparatory sketch for the

Immaculate Conception, now in the National Gallery in Dublin: he died suddenly on March 27, 1770, at the age of seventy-four. He was buried in the church of San Martín in Madrid. This was later demolished, so that even his tomb has vanished. The news of his death reached Venice a month later, on April 21. Of his sons, Lorenzo remained in Madrid, in a vain attempt to obtain the post of court painter; Giandomenico, however, immediately set off for Venice, arriving on November 12 of the same year.

*85. The Triumph of the
Pisani Family
2350x1350 cm
Stra (Venice), Villa Pisani*

*86. The Glory of Spain,
detail
Madrid, Royal Palace*

87. The Flight into Egypt by Boat
57x44 cm
Lisbon, Museu Nacional de Arte Antigua

88. The Rest on the Flight to Egypt
57x44 cm
Stuttgart, Staatsgalerie

Chronological Table

1696: Giambattista is born in Venice on March 5.

1697: his father Domenico dies on March 10.

1710: he enters the studio of Gregorio Lazzarini.

1715: he starts to paint the ornamental panels in the church of the Ospedaletto.

1716: he exhibits his study for the *Drowning of the Pharaoh* on the Feast Day of St. Rock (August 16).

1717: Tiepolo's name appears for the first time in the Fraglia, the guild of Venetian painters. Lovisa publishes the *Gran Teatro delle pitture e prospettive di Venezia*, containing four engravings based on drawings by Tiepolo.

1719: he secretly marries Cecilia Guardi on November 21.

1721: he is commissioned to paint the *Madonna del Carmelo*.

1722: he receives the commission for the *Martyrdom of Saint Bartholomew* for the church of San Stae.

1723: he enters the competition for the decoration of the chapel of San Domenico in the church of Santi Giovanni e Paolo, won by Piazzetta.

1724: Tiepolo paints an ornamental panel depicting the *Sacrifice of Isaac* to be set above the arch in the church of the Ospedaletto.

1726: he decorates the chapel of the Holy Sacrament in the cathedral of Udine and works in the castle; he begins work on the decoration of the Palazzo Patriarcale for Dionisio Dolfin. During the winter months he starts to paint the ten scenes from Roman history for the Dolfin family's palace in Venice.

1727: his son Giandomenico is born.

1730: he is in Milan (frescoes in Palazzo Archinto and Palazzo Casati).

1732: he delivers the altarpiece depicting *The Adoration of the Child* to the church of San Zulian.

1732-33: he works on the decoration of the Colleoni Chapel in Bergamo Cathedral.

1734: he frescoes some rooms in Villa Loschi at Vicenza; he delivers the Rovetta altarpiece.

1735: he signs and dates the *Madonna del Rosario*.

1736: his son Lorenzo is born. He turns down Count Tessin's invitation to go to Stockholm to decorate the palace of the king of Sweden.

1737: in January he consigns the *Martyrdom of Saint Agatha* to the basilica of Sant'Antonio in Padua; he goes to Milan to paint three frescoes in the basilica of Sant'Ambrogio. He also sends three altarpieces to Udine and paints the one for the altar of the Cornaro family in the Venetian church of San Salvador, now lost. He commences work on the fresco decoration of the church of the Gesuati, concluded in 1739.

1739: he paints the *Martyrdom of Saint Sebastian* for the monastic church of Diessen.

1740: he frescoes the ceiling of the gallery in Palazzo Clerici in Milan. He sends the altarpiece representing *The Appearance of the Virgin to Saint Philip Neri* to Camerino.

1743: he paints the *Apotheosis of Vettor Pisani* in Palazzo Pisani Moretta and the *Portrait of Antonio Riccobono* for the Accademia dei Concordi in Rovigo.

1743-44: frescoes in Villa Cordellina at Montecchio Maggiore.

1744: he consigns the eight lateral paintings for the ceiling of the Scuola Grande dei Carmini commissioned from him in 1739. He paints several canvases for the Dresden court, ordered from him by Francesco Algarotti.

1744-45: frescoes and canvases for Palazzo Barbarigo.

1745: between April and November he frescoes the vault of the church of the Scalzi, destroyed in 1915. In September he delivers the altarpiece depicting the *Martyrdom of Saint John* to Bergamo Cathedral.

1746-47: frescoes in Palazzo Labia in Venice.

1748: he paints two ceilings for Palazzo Manin in Venice, to celebrate the marriage of Ludovico Manin to Elisabetta Grimani. He consigns the altarpiece representing *Three Saints* to the church of the Gesuati.

1749: he sends the altarpiece depicting *Saint James the Greater* to Richard Wall, the Spanish ambassador in London. He delivers the central panel of the ceiling in the Scuola dei Carmini.

1750: on December 12 he leaves, with his sons Giandomenico and Lorenzo, for Würzburg, where he stays until 1753, working on the decoration of the Residenz.

1752: he finishes the frescoes in the Kaisersaal and starts on the one on the ceiling of the grand staircase.

1753: on November 8 he leaves Würzburg and returns to Venice.

1754: on May 8 he consigns the altarpiece representing *Saint John Nepomucenus* to the church of San Polo. He paints the frescoes in the church of the Pietà.

1757: he decorates Villa Valmarana and Palazzo Trento Valmarana in Vicenza with frescoes. Returning to Venice, he spends the last few months of the year working in Ca' Rezzonico.

1759: he delivers the altarpiece of the church of San Silvestro at Folzano on September 30 and the one for Este Cathedral on December 24. Between August and September he paints the frescoes in the oratory of the Purità at Udine, assisted by Giandomenico.

1760: he works for Tsarina Helena Petrovna. He is commissioned to paint the fresco in the salon of Villa Pisani at Stra.

1760-61: he works in Villa Pisani at Stra and Palazzo Canossa in Verona.

1762: on June 4 he reaches Madrid, accompanied by his sons Giandomenico and Lorenzo. He works on the decoration of three rooms in the Royal Palace until 1764.

1767-69: he paints the seven altarpieces for the church in Aranjuez.

1769: he is commissioned to decorate the collegiate church of Sant'Ildefonso at La Granja.

1770: he dies suddenly on March 27; he is buried in the church of San Martín in Madrid.

Bibliography

V. Da Canal, *Vita di Gregorio Lazzarini* (1732), edn. pub. by G. Moschini, Venice 1809

A.M. Zanetti, *Descrizione di tutte le pubbliche pitture della città di Venezia*, Venice 1733

Il Forestiere Illuminato, Venice 1740

A.M. Zanetti, *Della pittura veneziana...*, Venice 1771

L. Lanzi, *Storia pittorica della Italia*, Bassano 1795-96

F. Zanotto, *Storia della pittura veneziana*, Venice 1837

P. Gradenigo, *Notatori ed annali...*, edn. pub. by L. Livan, Venice 1942

P. Molmenti, *G.B. Tiepolo. La sua vita, le sue opere*, Milan 1909.

E. Sack, *Giambattista und Giandomenico Tiepolo*, Hamburg 1910.

G. Fogolari, *G.B. Tiepolo nel Veneto*, Milan 1913

G. Fiocco, *Tiepolo*, Florence 1926

Il Settecento Veneziano (catalogue of the exhibition), Venice 1929

A. Morassi, "The Young Tiepolo," in *The Burlington Magazine*, 1934

A. Morassi, "G.B. e G.D. Tiepolo alla Villa Valmarana," in *Le Arti*, 1941

R. Pallucchini, *Gli affreschi di Giambattista e Giandomenico Tiepolo alla Villa Valmarana di Vicenza*, Bergamo 1945

G. Lorenzetti, *Tiepolo* (catalogue of the exhibition in Venice), Venice 1951

G. Mazzariol and T. Pignatti, *Itinerario tiepolesco*, Venice 1951

T. Pignatti, *Tiepolo*, Verona 1951

A. Morassi, *G.B. Tiepolo*, London 1955

M.H. von Freeden and C. Lamb, *Tiepolo. Die Fresken der Würzburger Residenz*, Munich 1956

R. Pallucchini, *La pittura veneziana del Settecento*, Venice-Rome 1960

F. Haskell, *Patrons and Painters*, London 1963

E. Martini, *La pittura veneziana del Settecento*, Venice 1964

A. Morassi, *A Complete Catalogue of the Paintings of G.B. Tiepolo*, London 1965

T. Pignatti, *Tiepolo*, Brescia 1967

P. Zampetti, *Dal Ricci al Tiepolo* (catalogue of the exhibition in Venice), Venice 1967.

G. Knox, "Tiepolo and the Ceiling of the Scalzi," in *The Burlington Magazine* 1968

A. Pallucchini, *L'opera completa di Giambattista Tiepolo*, Milan 1968

F. Cessi, *Tiepolo*, Florence 1970

M. Precerutti Garberi, *Giambattista Tiepolo, gli affreschi*, Turin 1971

A. Rizzi, *Mostra del Tiepolo. I dipinti* (catalogue of the exhibition in Udine), Milan 1971

Atti del Congresso Internazionale di Studi sul Tiepolo (Udine 1970), Milan 1972

L. Moretti, "La data degli Apostoli della chiesa di San Stae," in *Arte veneta*, 1973

E. Martini, "I ritratti di Ca' Cornaro di Giovan Battista Tiepolo giovane," in *Notizie da Palazzo Albani*, 1974

A. Rizzi, *Tiepolo a Udine*, Udine 1974

F. Rusk Shapley, "Tiepolo's Zenobia Cycle," in *Hortus Imaginum. Essays in Western Art*, 1974

G. Knox, "The Tasso Cycles of Giambattista Tiepolo and Giannantonio Guardi," in *Museum Studies*, 1978

Gli affreschi nelle ville venete dal Seicento all'Ottocento, ed. by R. Pallucchini, Venice 1978

G. Knox, "Giambattista Tiepolo. Queen Zenobia and Ca' Zenobio: 'una delle sue prime fatture'", in *The Burlington Magazine*, 1979

M. Levey, *Painting in XVIII Century Venice*, London 1980

F. Buttner and W-Ch. von der Mulbe, *Giovanni Battista Tiepolo. Gli affreschi di Würzburg*, Milan 1981

E. Martini, *La pittura del Settecento veneto*, Maniago 1982

T. Pignatti, F. Pedrocco, and E. Martinelli Pedrocco, *Palazzo Labia a Venezia*, Turin 1982

A. Mariuz and G. Pavanello, "I primi affreschi di Giambattista Tiepolo," in *Arte Veneta*, 1985

C. Whistler, "A Modello for Tiepolo's Final Commission: the Allegory of Immaculate Conception," in *Apollo*, 1985

C. Whistler, "G.B. Tiepolo at the Court of Charles III," in *The Burlington Magazine*, 1986

S. Sponza, "Della decorazione pittorica della chiesa dell'Ospedaletto ed il problema della prima attività di Giambattista Tiepolo," in *Atti dell'Istituto Veneto di Scienze, Lettere ed Arti*, 1986-87

M. Levey, *Giambattista Tiepolo. La sua vita, la sua arte*, Milan 1988

Venezia e la Spagna, Milan 1988

W.L. Barcham, *The Religious Paintings of Giambattista Tiepolo*, Oxford 1989

M.E. Avagnina, F. Rigon, and R. Schiavo, *Tiepolo. Le ville vicentine*, Milan 1990

I Tiepolo e il Settecento vicentino (catalogue of the exhibition in Vicenza), Milan 1990

M. Gemin and F. Pedrocco, *Giambattista Tiepolo. I dipinti. Opera completa*, Venice 1993

R. Pallucchini, *La pittura nel Veneto. Il Settecento*, Milan 1994

Splendori del Settecento Veneziano (catalogue of the exhibition in Venice), Milan 1995

Index of Illustrations

The Great Masters of Art

Andrea del Sarto
Benozzo Gozzoli
Bernini
Botticelli
Bronzino
Brunelleschi
Canaletto
Caravaggio
Carpaccio
Cimabue
Correggio

Della Robbia
Domenico Ghirlandaio
Donatello
Duccio
Filippo Lippi
Fra Angelico
Giotto
Giovanni Bellini
Leonardo da Vinci
Luca Signorelli
Mantegna

Masaccio
Michelangelo
Piero della Francesca
Pietro and Antonio Lorenzetti
Pontormo/Rosso Fiorentino
Paolo Uccello/Domenico
Veneziano/Andrea del
Castagno
Raphael
Simone Martini
Titian

Forthcoming monographs:

Perugino
Pinturicchio